AMEN

Other books by Yehuda Amichai

Songs of Jerusalem and Myself
Poems
Not of This Time, Not of This Place

Amen

YEHUDA AMICHAI

**Translated from the Hebrew by
the author and Ted Hughes**

HARPER & ROW, PUBLISHERS
NEW YORK, HAGERSTOWN, SAN FRANCISCO, LONDON

Designed by Gloria Adelson

Library of Congress Cataloging in Publication Data

Amichai, Yehuda.
   Amen.
   Poems.
   I. Title.
PJ5054.A65A25   892.4'1'6   76–50164
ISBN 0–06–010090–7
ISBN 0–06–010089–3 pbk.

77 78 79 80 10 9 8 7 6 5 4 3 2

Contents

Introduction
by Ted Hughes

In 1966, when the first issue of the magazine
Modern Poetry In Translation was being prepared,
Daniel Weissbort, the Editor, found some translations
of the Israeli poet Yehuda Amichai and showed them
to me. We were both greatly intrigued and excited by
them. They eventually appeared, in that first issue, in
powerful company: Zbigniew Herbert, Miroslav
Holub, Vasko Popa. These poets were the same
generation as Amichai, early 1920s, and each one of
them had some claim to being among the dozen most
remarkable poets alive—a judgment that still holds
good after eleven years. It seemed to us that Amichai
shared their stature and something of their family
likeness. Nevertheless, he stood a little apart, and with
the passing of time it has become clearer just how
radically different he is. In 1966, it was already
noticeable that where the three poets from behind the
Iron Curtain gripped one's imagination and held
one's awe, somehow Amichai's verse attracted and
held one's affection as well. It became involved with
one's intimate daily experience in a curious way.

With this third volume of his translated poetry to
be published in the U.S., I am more than ever
convinced that here is one kind of poetry that
satisfies, for me, just about every requirement.

To appreciate what he manages to do, one has to imagine him as the chief character in a drama—chief in the sense that he is the one on whom we see the drama registering all its pressures. In this case, his speeches have the added authority that the role is real, and the drama is that crucial hinge of modern history—particularly the history of the West—which is the dilemma of modern Israel.

The forces on the move in this drama are for anybody to name. Even to such an outsider as myself, it as a matter of wonder to see such temperamental energies and traditions, from all the diverse corners of the diaspora, drawn back with the suddenness and violence of collision into that tiny patch of bare land, and there forced to combine and fight against what has repeatedly threatened to be not just defeat but extinction.

Every aspect of the situation is relevant to Amichai's poetry. The simplest assessment of the plot of the drama, and the dramatis personae, has to take account of the unique intensity of Jewish religious feeling, and its meaning for all Western Peoples. It has to take account of the Prophets, Biblical history, the supernatural world of Jewish mystical tradition, and the symbolic role of Israel itself, and in particular of Jerusalem. The accumulated inner strength and wealth of Jewish survival throughout the diaspora, and the peculiar election imposed on them by Hitler. The fact of the holocaust. The fact of the suddenly multiplying powers of the Arab world. A plot that enmeshes itself in a perpetual state of near-war, sudden wars, the threat of more and worse wars, endless future warfare while world powers shift the country this way and that like a pawn. It is clearly the drama of a war of survival on every level, the culmination of the long Jewish history of fighting for survival on every level, of a garrisoned last-stand people. At the same time, ironically, it is the story of a hectic modern Mediterranean holiday land, a tourist resort aswarm with nymphs and satyrs.

But this is only the start of the play. The plot now requires that this huge problem of spiritual inheritance and immediate physical challenge be solved, or at least dealt with in a practical way. And the character on whom this task has descended, the inheritor, the responsible man, the Prince Hamlet, is the modern Israeli citizen-soldier. But is he up to the job? This hero is not a full-time philosopher or general. The weird unmanageable fate has fallen on the shoulders of a man in the street, probably a schoolteacher, a conscript in all the wars, an ordinary individual who also happens to be in love. And that is what concerns him most, that he is in love.

This character's love poems, as the drama lurches along all round him, have been written by Yehuda Amichai.

Born in Germany—in Würzburg—in 1924, he moved to Palestine, with his family, in 1936, which was late in the day. The double perspective of this doubling of both homeland and language—at that most critical moment for both Hebrew and German— is the subject of his haunting novel, *Not of This Time, Not of This Place.* It is something perhaps that sets him apart from the Israelis born in Israel. But it makes him one of that archetypal generation of Jewish immigrants to Israel who survived the war, and who brought with them the whole accumulated experience of the diaspora to be counted over again and reappraised.

The dramatic role which Amichai has had to perform obviously demands unusual linguistic resources, for any adequate expression. Luckily for us who cannot read the Hebrew, he did not rest content with purely verbal means. What he has in common with Herbert, Holub, and Popa, is a language beyond verbal language, a language of images which operates with the complexity and richness of hieroglyphs. But the images are not drawn, in surrealist fashion, from the world of dreams. They are drawn, in Amichai's poetry, from the inner and outer history of Jewry. It is as if the whole ancient spiritual investment had been suddenly cashed, in a modern coinage, flooding his poetry with an inexhaustible currency of precise and weighty metaphors. Simultaneously, he has converted all the elements of modern Israeli circumstances to the same all-purpose coinage. And this is the language of his love poems. Nearly all his poems are love poems in one guise or another, many of them straightforwardly erotic—a modern Song of Songs, if one exists anywhere. But the particular nature of his bank of images introduces the complexity which is both just and true. Writing about his most private love pangs in terms of war, politics, and religion he is inevitably writing about war, politics, and religion in terms of his most private love pangs. And the large issues are in no wise diminished in this exchange. They are nowhere more real, more humanized and felt, than in these intimate, comical, sad poems— poems that become more and more life-size and warm and unforgettable the better we get to know them.

Each poem is like a telephone switchboard—the images operate lightning confrontations between waiting realities, a comic or terrible conversation between those heavy political or spiritual matters and the lovers.

This presence, within the actual texture of the writing, of the lived and deeply shared actuality of modern Israel, and of the human relationships determined by it, has steadily increased over the years in Amichai's poems. As they grow more open, simpler, and apparently more artless, they also grow more nakedly present, more close-up alive. They begin to impart the shock of actual events. No matter how mysterious or bizarre the mental leaps, the final effect is always one of a superior simplicity and directness. One is no longer so aware of the virtuosity of a dazzlingly gifted poet, but of a telling of real things he has lived and felt, without any literary self-consciousness, and in a poetry that seems once more the natural speech of people who speak about the psychological depth and density of such things candidly, humorously, generously. This is something so rare that I, for one, return to the poems again and again, and always find myself shaken, as by something truly genuine and alive.

The translations were made by the poet himself. All I did was correct the more intrusive oddities and errors of grammar and usage, and in some places shift about the phrasing and line endings. What I wanted to preserve above all was the tone and cadence of Amichai's own voice speaking in English, which seems to me marvelously true to the poetry, in these renderings. What Pound called the first of all poetic virtues—"the heart's tone." So as translations these are extremely literal. But they are also more, they are Yehuda Amichai's own English poems.

AMEN

Seven Laments for the Fallen
in the War

1

Mr. Beringer, whose son
fell by the Canal, which
was dug by strangers
for ships to pass through the desert,
is passing me at the Jaffa gate:

He has become very thin; has lost
his son's weight.
Therefore he is floating lightly
through the alleys,
getting entangled in my heart
like driftwood.

2

As a child he mashed potatoes
into golden purée.
After that one dies.

The living child has to be
cleaned after it returns from play.
But for the dead man
earth and sand are clear water

in which forever
he'll cleanse his flesh and purify.

3

The monument of the unknown soldier,
beyond, on the enemy's side.
A good target marker for the gunners
of future wars.

Or the war monument in London,
Hyde Park Corner, decorated
like a rich, splendid cake: one more
soldier raising head and rifle,
one more gun, another eagle, another
angel made of stone.

Whipped cream of a big marble flag
is poured over it all
with expert hand.

But the sugar-coated too-red
cherries
were eaten up already
by the gourmet of hearts. Amen.

4

I found an old textbook of animals,
Brehm, second volume, birds:
Description, in sweet language, of the lives
of crows, swallows and jays. A lot of mistakes
in Gothic printing, but a lot of love: "Our
feathered friends," "emigrate to warmer
countries," "nest, dotted egg, soft plumage,
the nightingale," "prophets of spring,"
The Red-Breasted Robin.

Year of printing 1913, Germany
on the eve of the war which became
the eve of all my wars.

My good friend, who died in my arms and in his
        blood
in the sands of Ashdod,* 1948, in June.

Oh, my friend,
red-breasted.

*Ashdod—a major battle in the Israeli War of Independence.

5

Dicky was hit,
like the water tower at Yad Mordecai*
was hit. A hole in his belly. Everything
poured out of him.

But he has remained thus, standing
in the landscape of my memory,
like the water tower at Yad Mordecai.
Not far from there he fell,
a little to the north, near Houleikat.†

6

Is all of this sorrow? I don't know.
I was standing in the cemetery, wearing
camouflage clothes of the living:
brown trousers and a shirt yellow as the sun.
Cemeteries are cheap and very undemanding.
Even wastebaskets are small, just
to hold thin wrapping paper of bought flowers.
Cemeteries are a well-behaved and disciplined thing.

*Yad Mordecai—a kibbutz in the south.
†Houleikat—a battlefield in the south.

"And I shall never forget you" written
on a little ceramic plate, in French.

I don't know who it is, that shall never forget;
he is even more unknown than the dead.
Is all of this sorrow? I think
so: "May you be comforted by the building of the
          land."

How much more can one build the land
to catch up in this terrible three-cornered contest
between comfort and building and death?

Yes, all this is sorrow. But leave
a little love burning, always,
as in a sleeping baby's room a little bulb,
without it knowing what the light is
and where it comes from. Yet it gives
a little feeling of security and silent love.

7

Memorial day for the war dead. Add now
the grief of all your losses to their grief,
even of a woman that has left you. Mix
sorrow with sorrow, like time-saving history,
which stacks holiday and sacrifice and mourning
on one day for easy, convenient memory.

Oh, sweet world soaked, like bread,
in sweet milk for the terrible toothless God.
"Behind all this some great happiness is hiding."
No use to weep inside and to scream outside.
Behind all this perhaps some great happiness is
          hiding.

Memorial day. Bitter salt is dressed up
as a little girl with flowers.
The streets are cordoned off with ropes,
for the marching together of the living and the dead.
Children with a grief not their own march slowly,
like stepping over broken glass.

The flautist's mouth will stay like that for many days.
A dead soldier swims above little heads

with the swimming movements of the dead,
with the ancient error the dead have
about the place of the living water.

A flag loses contact with reality and flies off.
A shopwindow is decorated with
dresses of beautiful women, in blue and white.
And everything in three languages:
Hebrew, Arabic and Death.

A great and royal animal is dying
all through the night under the jasmine
tree with a constant stare at the world.

A man whose son died in the war walks in the street
like a woman with a dead embryo in her womb.
"Behind all this some great happiness is hiding."

Poems from a cycle called
"Patriotic Songs"

1

Our baby was weaned in the first days
of the war. And I ran out to stare
at the terrible desert.

At night I came back again to see him
asleep. Already he's forgetting
his mother's nipples, and he'll go on forgetting
till the next war.

And so, while he was still small,
his hopes were closed, and his complaints
opened wide—never to close again.

2

The war broke out in autumn at the empty border
between sweet grapes and oranges.

The sky is blue, like veins in a woman's tormented
    thighs.

The desert is a mirror for those looking at it.

Sad males carry the memory of their families
in carriers and pouches and hunchback-knapsacks
and soul-bags and heavy eye-bladders.

The blood froze in its veins. That's why it can't be
        spilled,
but only broken into pieces.

3

October sun warms our faces.
A soldier is filling bags with soft sand
in which once he played.

October sun warms our dead.
Sorrow is a heavy wooden board.
Tears are nails.

4

I have nothing to say about the war,
nothing to add. I'm ashamed.

All the knowledge I have absorbed in my life

I give up, like a desert
which has given up all water.
Names I never thought I would forget
I'm forgetting.

And because of the war I say again,
for the sake of a last and simple sweetness:
The sun is circling round the earth. Yes.
The earth is flat, like a lost, floating board. Yes.
God is in Heaven. Yes.

5

I've shut myself in. I'm like
a heavy, tight swamp. I sleep war
like hibernation.

They've made me a commander of the dead
on the Mount of Olives.

Always, even in victory,
I lose.

7

The blood erecting the penis
is not semen.

And blood spilled, of course,
is not semen.

And semen drowning in blood is not semen
and blood without semen is nothing
and semen without blood is nil.

8

What has the dead burned man bequeathed to us?
What does the water want us to do?

To make no noise, to keep it clean,
to behave very quietly at its side,
to let it flow.

10

I sometimes think about my fathers
and their forefathers from the destruction

of the temple onward through medieval tortures
until me.
I only remember as far back as my grandfather:
He did not have any additional hands,
or a special plug, or a spare navel,
or any instruments to receive and pass on to me.

He was a village Jew, God-fearing
and heavy-eyed. An old man
with a long pipe. My first memory
is of my grandmother with trembling hands
spilling a kettle of boiling water over my feet
when I was two.

11

The town I was born in was destroyed by shells.
The ship in which I sailed to the land of Israel was
      drowned later in the war.

The barn at Hammadia where I had loved was burned
      out.
The sweet shop at Ein-Gedi was blown up by the
      enemy.
The bridge at Ismailia, which I crossed to and fro on

the eve of my loves,
has been torn to pieces.

Thus my life is wiped out behind me according to an
    exact map:

How much longer can my memories hold out?

The girl from my childhood was killed and my father
    is dead.

That's why you should never choose me
to be a lover or a son, or a bridge-crosser
or a citizen or a tenant.

15

Even my loves are measured by wars:
I am saying this happened after the Second
World War. We met a day before the
Six-Day War. I'll never say
before the peace '45–'48 or during
the peace '56–'67.

But knowledge of peace
passes from country to country,
like children's games,
which are so much alike, everywhere.

16

A song of lovers in Jerusalem: we are
included in most of the prophecies of wrath
and in almost all of the good messages.

We are to be found on picture postcards
of our city. Perhaps we can't be seen
because we were sitting in a house
or too small;
the picture was taken from
a passing airplane.

18

The graves in Jerusalem are gates
of deep tunnels on the day of their opening—
after which they stop digging.

The tombstones are beautiful
cornerstones of buildings
that will never be built.

21

Jerusalem is a place where all remember
that they have forgotten something
but they don't remember what.

And for the sake of this remembering
I wear my father's face on mine.

That is the city where the containers of my
        dreams
fill up as with ocean divers' oxygen.
Its holiness
turns sometimes into love.

And questions which are asked
among these hills have remained unchanging:
Have you seen my flock? Have you
seen my shepherd?

And the door of my house is open
like a tomb
out of which somebody is resurrected.

24

They are burning the photographs
of divided Jerusalem, and those
beautiful love letters of a silent love.

The big whole lady is back,
noisy with gold and copper and stones
for fat and legal life.

But I don't like her.
Sometimes I remember the quiet one.

25

An old gym teacher is broiling
in the sun by the wall. His shoes
are being shined far away
from his head. And high above,
longings stir like rustling paper.

I never realized gym teachers
could be sad. He is very tired
and wants nothing more than
that the beautiful tourist girl sitting
beside him at a table will get up before him
and walk about with
her wobbling round buttocks,
which she has brought with her from her countries.
He wants nothing more.

28

Oh, who has the quietest face here?
Thus rings the bell from Mount Zion.

What goes to the holy hill of Moriah?
Children go with their parents on Sabbath,
eating rotten almonds and decaying chocolate bars.

Who has not cleaned the table?
Kings and generals and prophets too,
who were playing dice on the table of Jerusalem
and scattered them all over the world.

Who ever saw Jerusalem naked?
Even archaeologists never did.
Because she never stripped completely.
She always put on new houses
instead of the worn and torn and broken.

29

People travel far away to say:
this reminds me of some other place.
That's like it was, it's similar. But
I knew a man who traveled to New York
to commit suicide. He argued that the houses
in Jerusalem are not high enough and that everyone
        knows him.

I remember him with love, because once
he called me out of class in the middle of a lesson:
"There's a beautiful woman waiting for you outside in
        the garden,"
and he quieted the noisy children.

When I think about the woman and about the
        garden

I remember him on that high rooftop,
the loneliness of his death and the death of his
        loneliness.

33

A song of my homeland: The knowledge
of its waters starts with tears.

Sometimes I love water, sometimes stone.
These days I'm more in favor of stones.
But this might change.

34

Let the memorial hill remember, instead of me,
that's his job. Let the park in memory remember
let the street names remember
let the famous building remember
let the house of worship in the name of God
        remember
let the rolling scrolls of the law remember
let memorial services remember, let the flags
        remember

those multicolored shrouds of history (the
corpses they wrapped have anyhow turned to dust),
let dust remember, let dung remember
at the gate, let afterbirth remember.

Let the wild beasts and the sky's birds eat and
        remember.
Let all of them remember, so that I can rest.

35

In summer, peoples of different nations
visit each other
to smell out
each other's weak, sweet spots.

Hebrew and Arabic,
which are like stones of the tongue and sand of the
        throat,
have softened for tourists like oil.

Jeehad and holy wars
burst like figs.

Water pipes of Jerusalem protrude
like veins and tendons of an old, tired man.

Its houses are like teeth in the lower jaws
grinding in vain,
because heavens are empty above.

Perhaps Jerusalem is a dead city
in which people
move and wriggle like worms.

Sometimes they have big festivities.

36

Every night God takes his glittering
merchandise out of his showcase—
holy chariots, tables of law, fancy beads,
crosses and bells—
and puts them back into dark boxes
inside and pulls down the shutters: "Again,
not one prophet has come to buy."

37

All those stones, all this sorrow,
all this light, debris of night hours, ash of noon,
all those twisted pipes of holiness,
wall and towers, rusty halos,
all prophecies which couldn't hold back, like old men,
all sweaty wings of angels, all
stinking candles, all this false tourism,
dung of redemption, bliss and testicles,
garbage of nothingness, bomb and time.

All this dust, all these dead bones
in the process of resurrection and of wind,
all this love, all these
stones, all this sorrow.

Fill up with them all the valleys around
so that Jerusalem will be a flat place
for my sweet airplane, to come
and take me up there.

A Majestic Love Song

You are beautiful, like prophecies,
And sad, like those which come true,
Calm, with the calmness afterward.
Black in the white loneliness of jasmine,
With sharpened fangs: she-wolf and queen.

With a very short dress, in fashion,
But weeping and laughter from ancient times,
Perhaps from some book of other kings.
I've never seen foam at the mouth of a war horse,
But when you lathered your body with soap
I saw.

You are beautiful, like prophecies
That never come true.
And this is the royal scar;
I pass over it with my tongue
And with pointed fingers over that sweet
        roughness.

With hard shoes you knock
Prison bars to and fro around me.

Your wild rings
Are the sacred leprosy of your fingers.

Out of the earth emerge
All I wished never to see again:
Pillar and window sill, cornice and jug, broken pieces
　　　of wine.

There is so much face hiding here
(Whose from whose?)
And at night, to stir with that
Blind golden scepter
In pleasures.
With the weight of kingdom and tiredness.

Outing at Some Beautiful Place

With a Jewish girl
Who has American hope
In her eyes and whose nostrils are still
Very sensitive to anti-Semitism.

"Where did you get those eyes?"
Eyes like those one does not receive at birth—
So much color, so much sadness.

She wore the coat of a soldier, discharged
Or dead—by victory or defeat—
In some worn-out war.

"On a bonfire of burned letters
It is impossible to cook even one cup of coffee."

After that to continue walking
To some beautiful, hidden place
At which a wise and experienced field commander
Would have put his mortars.

"In summer, after you, this hill
Gets covered by a soft thought."

A Bride Without Dowry

A bride without dowry with a deep navel
In her tanned belly. A little hole
For food and drink, for birds.

Oh, yes, this is the bride with her big buttocks
Surprised out of her dreams and her fat
In which she had bathed naked
Like Susanna and the Elders.

Oh, yes, this is this serious girl
With freckles. What's the meaning
Of an upper lip pushing itself over the lower!
Dark drinking and laughter,
Little sweet animal, Monique.

And she has a will of iron
Inside a body of soft and spoiled flesh:
What a terrible blood bath
Is she preparing for herself,
What a terrible Roman arena streaming with blood.

Love Song

It started like this: In the heart it became
loose and easy and happy, as
when someone feels his bootlaces loosening a bit
and bends down.

After this came other days.

Now I'm like a Trojan Horse
filled with terrible loves:
Each night they break out and run amok
and at dawn they come back
into my dark belly.

Once a Great Love

Once a great love cut my life in two.
The first part goes on twisting
at some other place like a snake cut in two.

The passing years have calmed me
and brought healing to my heart and rest to my eyes.

And I'm like someone standing in
the Judean desert, looking at a sign:
"Sea Level."
He cannot see the sea, but he knows.

Thus I remember your face everywhere
at your "face level."

Song

When a man is abandoned by
his love, an empty round space
expands inside him like a cave
for wonderful stalagmites, slowly.

Like the empty space
in history, kept open for
Meaning and Purpose and tears.

Love Song

Heavy and tired with a woman on a balcony:
"Stay with me." Roads die like people:
Quietly or suddenly breaking.
Stay with me. I want to be you.
In this burning country
Words have to be shade.

Love Song

People use each other
as a healing for their pain. They put each other
on their existential wounds,
on the eye, on the cunt, on mouth and open hand.
They hold each other hard and won't let go.

Little Song of Tranquillity

If wandering is quicker than death
What is there to fear?

You have two hands and two feet—
You are not lonely.

Beautiful bodies are folded around their love
With the folding skill and wisdom of nursery schools.

A man passes through the wall
And the wall remains whole and he remains whole.

Such a man you are—
Or you will become one.

The Portuguese Synagogue in Amsterdam

What tourists are those?
Dark dogs of memory throw their darkness at them.
Without payment they enter the synagogue,
With black paper skullcaps
Which they have taken from a box at the gate.
Gilded atonements turn silently from the ceiling
Over empty benches with no sinners in them, or sin.
Leftovers of prayers stick to the walls
Like the crust of limestone in an old kettle.

Who are they, that have come from waterless places
And have become crossers of many bridges
In countries whose railway stations' names
Are always "Entrance" or "Exit"?
After that they liquidate meat
In restaurants with knife and fork
With sad table manners.

Who are they? Sometimes one of them
In a moment of calm absent-mindedness
Will look at his wrist to see time,
But there is no watch.

"I think that a return ticket
Is a very exciting thing," the woman said,
"And full of promising love."

The Synagogue in Florence

Tender spring in the courtyard,
A tree blossoming, four girls playing
Between two lessons of the sacred language
In front of a memorial wall
Made of marble: Levi, Sonino, Cassuto
And others
In straight lines, as in a newspaper
Or in the scrolls of the Torah.

The tree stands there in memory of nothing
But of this spring.
A rivederci, our father.
Buona notte, our king.

Tears at the eye.
Like dry crumbs in a pocket
Of some past cake.

Buona notte, Sonino.
A rivederci, the six million,
The girls, the tree and the crumbs.

The Synagogue in Venice

This synagogue knows of all the many waters
That cannot put out this love.

I cover my head with my arm,
Which comes out of my shoulder, not far from my
      heart.

No need for a skullcap. Many thanks. This
Is a museum. This is an empty grave
Of those who rose out of it
For resurrection or new death.

No need for beautiful glass jewelry
From the island of Murano. This multicolored
Blowing-up is the terrible cancer
Of glass and memory.
One window for dim light is enough.

After that to be very quiet
Like a buoy at the water's gate,
To warn of gold and of love
And of days of youth never returning—

A head of longing afloat and bobbing slowly
On all the many and torpid waters.

I Have Many Dead

I have many dead buried in the air.
I have a bereaved mother, although I'm still alive.

I am like space
making war against time.

Once the green color was very happy
behind your face at the window.
Only in my dreams I still love strongly.

I Have Become Very Hairy

I have become very hairy all over my body.
I'm afraid they'll start hunting me because of my fur.

My multicolored shirt has no meaning of love—
it looks like an air photo of a railway station.

At night my body is open and awake under the
      blanket,
like eyes under the blindfold of someone to be shot.

Restless I shall wander about;
hungry for life I'll die.

Yet I wanted to be calm, like a mound with all its
      cities destroyed,
and tranquil, like a full cemetery.

On My Return

I will not be greeted on my return
by children's voices, or by the barking
of a loyal dog, or by blue smoke rising
as it happens in legends.

There won't happen for me any "and he
lifted his eyes"—as
in the Bible—"and behold."

I have crossed the border of being an orphan.
It's a long time since they called me
an ex-serviceman.
I'm not protected anymore.

But I have invented the dry weeping.
And who has invented this
has invented the beginning of the world's end,
the crack and the tumbling down and the end.

My Father's Memorial Day

On my father's memorial day
I went out to see his mates—
All those buried with him in one row,
His life's graduation class.

I already remember most of their names,
Like a parent collecting his little son
From school, all of his friends.

My father still loves me, and I
Love him always, so I don't weep.
But in order to do justice to this place
I have lit a weeping in my eyes
With the help of a nearby grave—
A child's. "Our little Yossy, who was
Four when he died."

A Man for Play

They have acquired an old car
For the playground of a kindergarten
And painted it yellow and red.

They will acquire me too for grownups:
In my own courtyard
I'll be put up for show, in beautiful colors,
A man for play and useful studies.

The few words left to say
I can attach to a cough and a sneeze.

Sometimes you never know
A man's year of birth
Until he is dead.

"So that your days will lengthen upon the earth":
As if it were possible to lengthen them
In both directions—even the one before birth.

A Song About Rest

Show me a land whose women are more beautiful
than those on its posters,
and whose gods lay good things
around my eye, on my forehead and my painful nape.

"Never again will I find rest for my soul."
Each day a new last day passes,

and I must still return
to those places where they measure me
with trees grown since and all that has been
        destroyed.

I stamp my feet and shuffle my shoes
to get rid of what has stuck to me:
Dung of my soul, dirt of emotion, sand of love.

"Never again will I find rest for my soul."
Let me sit in the revolving chair
of an A.A. gunner, of a pianist,
of a barber, and I shall turn round and round
restfully until my end.

My Soul

There is a great battle raging, for my mouth
not to harden and for my jaws
not to become like heavy doors
of an iron safe, so that my life
may not be called pre-death.

Like a newspaper clinging to a fence in the blowing
      wind,
so my soul clings to me.
If the wind stops, my soul will fall.

Lost in Grace

Lost in grace
like a foot in a too big shoe.

The little hole burned in my shirt
is an additional eye for me to see through.

What are you bringing with you, to sleep?
A sleep and a pink cushion, embraced.

The bicycle wheels of my older son
turn around all night. I don't sleep.

The yellow plastic fish of my little son
smiles always.

Loneliness has windows and a door.
It has pipes outside and inside, like any house.

And what's ahead of me is big
and calm, like the still, empty space in a cemetery.

Quiet Joy

I am standing at a place where once I loved.
The rain is falling. The rain is my home.

I think in words of longing
A landscape as far as I can hold.

I remember you waving your hand,
Like wiping white mist from a windowpane.

And your face, as if enlarged
From an old, much-blurred photograph.

Once I did great injustice
To myself and to others.

But the world is made beautifully and built
For a good rest, like a bench in a park.

So I have found now
A quiet joy, too late,
Like finding out a dangerous malady too late:

A few months more for quiet joy.

A Young Jerusalem Poet

Behind the partition made of bookshelves
His wife sleeps at eleven in the morning.
That's why I shall hold back my bitterness
And speak silently, whisper honey.

A young man and so serious—
Until his cheeks have become like reins:
Where is he riding to—this Eye-rider?

His first wife was a light bird,
Peeping and twittering through the same books.

This sleeping one is his second one, and quiet,
Surrounded by big wine, but
Very sober in the midst of it,
A lazy sun at ease.

He goes out into the streets
To fight for the law
Of immunity for lovers.

Song to a Friend

You do not sleep at night, you say
The hard bouncing ball of insomnia knocks wildly
Inside you all night through
In a game without a way out.

I don't sleep either sometimes—but for
Different reasons. Another forgetting
Opens and closes for us
In houses far from each other,
A face weeping at my window is laughing
At your window, but it's the same sleep
That won't come to either of us.
We are both unhappy lovers
Of the same sleep.

Now you are a man successful and suffering.
Already your eyes show
The same dark process of becoming
Hunter and hunted

In one body. You eat partridges
Drenched in monastery wines
With sad slowness. And I am a man
Eating quickly
In moments of resting
Between two escapes. And the heart

With its hasty loves, like a tongue burned:
Forgetting the taste in sudden pain
And after that forgetting the pain too.

Now you are a man with a black beard.
This is a beard of mourning* for the
Death of childhood among citrus groves.
Too late you remembered to mourn for it.

But sometimes you are a sun of black hair
And in your eyes
There is still something like a signaling
To a happiness far away.

*A Jewish custom in mourning the death of a relative is to refrain from shaving for thirty days.

Letter of Recommendation

On summer nights I sleep naked
in Jerusalem on my bed,
which stands on the brink
of a deep valley
without rolling down into it.

During the day I walk about,
the Ten Commandments on my lips
like an old song someone is humming to himself.

Oh, touch me, touch me, you good woman!
This is not a scar you feel under my shirt.
It's a letter of recommendation, folded,
from my father:
"He is still a good boy and full of love."

I remember my father waking me up
for early prayers. He did it caressing
my forehead, not tearing the blanket away.

Since then I love him even more.
And because of this
let him be woken up
gently and with love
on the Day of Resurrection.

The Candles Went Out

The candles went out
And so there won't be any cause
For my eyes to moisten.
Eternity jumps at me like a dog
With dry barking.

In order to ease pressure on me,
I lure my blood
Into digesting and fornicating
So it will be dispersed
In my intestines and penis
And not make painful thoughts in my head.

And in the days of my childhood and nights of love
I've hidden mines of truth.
But my grown-up days
Have burned the maps.
That's why I live precariously in lies,
Or don't go out at all.

Once again, pictures become more and more,
Words become less,
As in a children's book.
So the circle closes.

Ideal Love

To start love like this: with the shot of a gun
Like Ramadan.*
That's a religion! Or with the blowing of a ram's
     horn,
As at the High Holidays, to exorcise sins.
That's a religion! That's a love!

Souls—to the front!
To the firing line of eyes.
No hiding back in the white navel.
Emotions—out of the fat belly, forward!
Emotions out for close combat!

But let's keep the route to childhood open—
As even the most victorious army
Always leaves itself a retreat open.

*Ramadan—the Moslem month of fasting.

A Song About a Photograph

It's sad in this photograph of the forest
Just before spring. Bare trees penetrate slowly
Into my soul. Yesterday's rustle at my feet.
But the words "before daybreak" are still
Sweet in my ears and soft
Like the inner side of a prophecy.

At midday my voice rose like a sudden gust of wind.
I bought myself a suitcase with a zipper
For my journey. My God, what else
Does a man buy for himself while he's alive,
As well as shroud and tombstone?

I washed my hands before a mirror and I knew
He that has created man has created death.
And out of five who were once together
Only three remain, and are scattered.

God will bring the dead back to life, maybe,
But he won't put torn things together
Nor will he close the cracks.
Even the one in the street in front of your home
Will get longer and widen into the world.

A Memory Advancing into the Future

I am standing now in the landscape
Which we both looked at from the hillock:
Trees swaying in the wind
Like people swaying at the Apocalypse.

The happiness of their near distance
Was unbearable. We said what a
Pity we don't have more time. "If we
Come here next time, we'll go there."

I'm there.
I have time enough.
I'm the next time.

A Dog After Love

After you left me
I let a dog smell at
My chest and my belly. It will fill its nose
And set out to find you.

I hope it will tear the
Testicles of your lover and bite off his penis
Or at least
Will bring me your stockings between his teeth.

The Day I Left

The day I left, spring broke out
to fulfill what had been said: darkness, darkness.

We had a meal together. They spread a white
      tablecloth
for tranquillity. They put a candle for candle's sake.

We ate and we knew: The fish's soul
is his empty bones.

We stood once more by the sea:
Someone else already had made and filled everything.

And love—those few nights
like rare stamps. The touching of the heart
without leaving it hurt.
I travel lightly, like prayers of Jews,
rise simply like rising eyes and like
a flight to some other place.

To Speak About Changes Was to Speak Love

It's a long time since I have heard from you.
I have not received even a little piece of paper,
even like an official one from offices,
which have forgotten my name and my existence.

The generation machine is still sweet
between my thighs, but for a long time
I haven't felt the sweetness of a letter between my
      eyes.

We did not stay long enough together
to put us up as a lovers' monument.

Now time comes in place of time.
Sadness is changing its people like clothes
and your serious face is slicing your life:
each slice with another man on it.

Once we were talking about changes.
To speak about changes was to speak love.

Pain of Being Far Away

Pain of being far away
cuts my heart, as a sweet fruit is cut.
But where are the good tears!

Fog covers the house on the hill
at morning. People in it
say: Fog covers the whole world.

There are great longings
like someone who wakes up
in a bed in which he didn't fall asleep.

At noon I sent flowers
from a flower shop at the station:
On a little card I wrote words of good luck and
        passing love
with a pencil chained like a dog.

But where are the good tears,
the keys, the bunch of keys, of the face.

No One Puts His Hope

No one puts his hope on me.
Dreams of others are closed before me:
I'm not in them.

Even the voices in the room
are a sign of desolation, like cobwebs.

The loneliness of the body
which has room for a few more bodies.

Now they are taking each other's loves
down from the shelf. Until it's empty.

And outer space begins.

Sometimes I'm Very Happy and Desperate

Sometimes I'm very happy and desperate.
Then I'm stuck deeply
in the fleece
of the world-sheep,
like a tick.
I'm happy so.

The Song of My Father's Cheeks

My father's cheeks when he was my age were soft
Like the velvet bag which held his praying shawl.

The last cups of Kiddush* which he drank
Drank his beautiful face.

May he that doesn't believe me see
The quiet cup which remained with us.

I want to start anew
With graying hair and nights clean of dreams.

But my mother and my sister threw stones at me from
      the field,
Which have become precious stones in my flesh.

By day I skid in the black afterbirth of history,
At night I cry "God!" out of the sack.

May he that doesn't believe me come and see me
Like revisiting an old battlefield.

May he that doesn't believe me
Come back from the dead and see it is so.

*Kiddush—the blessing of the wine at holiday meals.

We Were Near

We were so near to each other,
like two numbers in a lottery,
just one cipher apart.
One of us will win, perhaps.

Beautiful are your face and your name,
printed on you as on a tin of a
marvelous preserve:
Fruit and its name.
Are you still inside?

Time will come, when days will be
sweet as nights
and beautiful for people
to whom time will be unimportant.

Then we shall know.

Take Me to the Airport

Take me to the airport:
I don't fly, I don't go,
I don't leave.
But take me to a white airplane
among the gray mists of olive trees.

Say words which change
seasons in the great urge
of the hour of departing.

Then hands will come
to the weeping eyes
as to a trough
and drink and drink.

Love Poem in California

People who leave their house
Turn it into a house of prayer.
Its door is made of thick wood with a strong bolt,
But the window is big and vulnerable.
On the table a comb stuck into a hairbrush,
The only reminder of two together in love,
A bookmark made of paper, but no book,
A mirror and no face. But your name!

I am smoking here, Diane,
In your cottage, so that the smoke will stay inside the
      cracks,
Because my words will not stay.

You have now many addresses,
Like a bouquet of multicolored flowers.
Yet you are in a season in which hunting is outlawed:
It is forbidden to love you
Now, and to search.

We are so far from each other.
You too do not live before Christ or after,
But aside and on your own. Here too
First love is fixing stubbornly,
The rest of your life.

"Because as rain and snow fall
From heaven and never return there"*
They will, and they will return. They didn't
Know it then.

In the days when your past will become my future,
We shall be beautiful, each one separate.
Beautiful like the streaming waters
Of your place, Diane,
And like the vast standing desert of mine.

*A quotation from the Prophet Isaiah.

Four Poems About People

1

So I met people from my past: "You are
From another layer. You are a different learning.
Your head belongs to some different place. Your hand
Is stretched out from there. You've forgotten
That eyes cannot hold anything,
But just see."

This is a question of melting
Of one material in another,
A face melting in night and mist,
Words melting in time,
Staying there dissolved.

These are home-lost people.
Their house has left them—
Not all at once, but each stone at its time,
Each tile, each curtain, each word.

And the shape of forgetting
Is like lips closed, humming.

2

Nothing to be angry about, nothing to be afraid of:

You sit in a public park in an abandoned gun post
From which a long-ago enemy once viewed you
In the sweet last light of a khamsin day.*

The rustling of wind in the trees again discovers
Silence in you. The heart sometimes answers
From far off, like dogs
From villages scattered over the mountains.

You have become a shepherd
And sheep and pasture all in one body.
You are tired, like children after a marvelous outing,
And you find out that the difference
Between a well, dug by man,
And a spurting spring
Is not great.
Everything is interconnected in the time of water.

*Khamsin—a hot desert wind.

3

And so you find yourself always standing
Between the much-praised landscape
And the one that praises it and explains it
To those standing around him in an enthralled circle.

You don't interfere anymore.
And words, not meant for you,
Are divided again by your body
Like wind, like water being combed,
And close again beyond you.

Sweet atheism still blossoms
Around here among rocks
With a lonely and desperate smell, like
The blossoming of the first belief in one God.

The mountainside cut by iron
Will again turn yellow and tan in summer
And be covered with grass, next spring
To be like any mountain at springtime,

Like my side, from which you were cut away
Some years ago.

4

There is a bird in the sky
Which, perhaps, is singing now
A sweet song:

If only I were a human being,
A man with feet
On this great and heavy earth,
I would stand and stand and stand
And never move from there.

I Dreamt About You

I dreamt about you. My dream was like
a great vaulted worry inside a railway station
hall in London. Suddenly
your face was there
with its night and its faraway sleep.

Young and beautiful people asked questions and filled
        in forms
about the destinations of the travelers.
Trains went and wet wires accompanied
those who needed them along the way.

I remember you happy: you were like children
in front of a sweet shop, just pointing:
This, this and this.

In those days I read only Present in your palms
and your face: no other tense.

And what has been will be again
and what has not yet been will be, will be.

Only you, whose face can be likened now
to a window in a receding house, never again.

Sadness of the Eyes and Descriptions
of a Journey

There is a dark memory on which the noise of
Playing children is scattered like powdered sugar.

There are things which will never again
Protect you and there are doors stronger than tombs.

There is a melody like the one in Ma'adi,
Near Cairo—with a promise of things
Which the silence of now
Tries to keep, in vain.

And there is a place to which you can never return.
A tree hides it during the day
And a lamp lights it up at night.
And I can't say any more
And I don't know anything else.

To forget and blossom, to blossom and forget, is all.
The rest is sadness of the eyes and descriptions of a
      journey.

To a Convert

Abraham's son learns to be a Jew.
He wants to be one very quickly.
Do you know what you are doing?
What's the hurry? After all, a man is not
a fig tree: everything, all together. Leaves
and fruit and buds—everything. (Yet the fig tree
is a Jewish tree.)

Aren't you afraid of the pain of circumcision?
Are you sure they won't go on
circumcising you until nothing is left
but sweet Jew pain?

I know: you want to be a baby again.
To be carried around on an embroidered cushion,
to be passed on from woman to woman,
mothers and godmothers
with big breasts and bellies. You want the
scent of perfume in your nose and the taste
of sweet wine for the little sucking mouth.

Now you are at the hospital: resting and healing.
Women wait outside under your window for your
        foreskin.
The one who catches it first—you'll be hers forever.

My Mother and Me

For many years now you have suffered
this khamsin, each year twice.

For nine months you carried me in your body.
For one year you carried me outside on your arm.
Oh, how much my face looks now like your arm,
how much my soul is like the tormented
skin of your bandaged feet.
How much has the khamsin made us alike
and both of us like this land.

And on the Day of Atonement, 1948,
you gave me cake, when I came
for a short and silent hour, to sit with you
in these rooms, on my way
back to the Negev desert,
a cake to eat after the fast, a cake
to be covered with dust, a cake for the
battle of Beersheba, a cake for the crumbs
to help me to find my way back from death.

Near the new park, in what was no man's land,
I saw fresh brown earth brought from afar.
And I saw empty tins, which once
held saplings of trees, now rusty and torn.

I do not know who has remained to love us.
I ask myself, how many people
would be ready to demonstrate for me,
or to stage a hunger strike for you at the walls?

I put on sandals, which cleave
my foot like the hoof of an ox.
You too sometimes still walk
festive Jerusalem with your aching feet.

But you and I are losing
free movements. The place
becomes too wide around us and superfluous.
And the eye's pupil stays fixed: not for sleep.

Into God's closed book
we shall be put, and there we shall rest
to mark for him the page where he stopped reading.

Today My Son

Today my son sold
Roses at a coffeehouse in London.
He approached the table
I was sitting at with merry friends.

His hair is gray. He is older than me.
But he is my son.
He says perhaps
I know him.
He was my father.

My heart broke in his chest.

Dennis Was Very Sick

Dennis was very sick.
His face retreated
But his eyes advanced from it
With great courage,
As in a war
When the fresh reinforcements
Pass on their way to the front
The retreating columns of the beaten.

He has to get healthy soon.
He is like our bank,
In which we deposited all we had in our heart.
He is like Switzerland,
Filled with banks.

Already he is smoking one cigarette,
Trembling a little,
And as it should be with a true poet,
He puts the burned matches
Back into the box.

To Remember Is a Kind of Hope

The speed of distance between us:
Not that one went away while the other stayed,
but the double speed of two going from each other.

Of the house I destroyed, not even the broken pieces
      are mine anymore.
And, once, all the words we wanted to say to each
      other
during our lives were stacked in straight clean heaps
of window frames at a new building site,
while we were still silent.

I don't know what happened to you since,
and whatever happened to me
I don't know how it happened.
To remember is a kind of hope.

Harlem, a Dead Story

At the Harmonie café, Rotterdam,
one last evening. His hand
resting between her thighs,
her hands on the table,
beautiful and pale,
like disillusioned
idealists.

The washrooms are in the basement,
white and very quiet.
You went down there and wept
after so many years, again.
It seemed you had been here before
and you realize, suddenly,
you have.

So you bring yourself to the train.
You are all right.
The little courtyard in Jerusalem
was a mistake,
Harlem,
a dead story.

He Who Forgets

He who forgets one
forgets three: Him
and the name of his street
and the one whose name is that of the street.

You don't have to weep.
There were two eucalyptus trees.
They certainly have grown. It was
toward night then. You don't have to weep.

And all is quiet now
and right and sensible and a little sad,
like a father who is raising his little child by himself,
like a little child growing alone with his father.

Ruth, What Is Happiness?

Ruth, what is happiness? We should have
talked about it, but we didn't.
The efforts we make to look happy
take our strength, as from tired soil.

Let's go home. To different homes.
"And in case we don't see each other anymore."

Your bag slung over your shoulder
made you an efficient wanderer
without symmetry, with bright eyes.

When the wind, lifting clouds,
will lift my heart as well and
bring it to another place—
that's true happiness.

"And in case we don't see each other anymore."

Menthol Sweets

Inside names nestle little animals.
Flowers grow out of what never will be again.

And a hand has written "Open" on a closed gate
And drawn eyes on blind places.

The head faces in the opposite direction
To the so-much-loved landscape.

"I'm a great believer in menthol sweets"
She said weeping bitterly and went her way.

Gone Are the Days of Night

Gone are the days of night, whose sweet shades
were like the colors of ripening fruits, gone
and returning to others. He who put
masculine and feminine into language put
into it also departing.

And you are like the one who swore to return each
      year at that time.
You are blue inside and brown outside, like vows,
and your words are exact, like shades of grass blades
      on the dunes.

In a Leap Year

In a leap year the day of death gets nearer or
farther away from the day of birth.
Grapes are filled with pain.
Their juice is thickened, like sweet human semen.

And I am like a man who by day
passes the places he dreamed about at night.
A sudden scent brings back to me
what long years of silence
made me forget. The blossoms of the acacia
at the beginning of the rainy season
and sands long buried under houses.

Now, all I can still do is
darken in the evening.
I am happy with what I have. And all I still
want to say is my name and
the place I come from, and perhaps my father's name,
like prisoners of war who are permitted
to say only this and no more,
according to the Geneva Convention.

She Told Me Not to Come

She told me not to come anymore
Into her recess room, that
It caused her grief. A young man
Was sitting there with a beautiful face, his nose
    straight
Like a Greek's and my nose big with nostrils excited
    like a bird.

Once I gave her a name
Like a botanist giving a name to a rare flower he has
    found.
She told me not to come anymore. Her skin
Was aglow and tanned. "A skin like that
Protects only from sun rays, not from pain."

"You sow walls everywhere. You plant
High walls. Your end will never meet
Your beginning." A young man was there
Who did not call her by her name.
They lay silently. Wine was rolling
Outside: Blessed be the one that has made
The fruit of the vine.

And I: Blessed he that has made
The fruit of the end.

A Mutual Lullaby

A long time ago I wanted to tell you to sleep.
But your eyes won't let sleep come; your thighs won't,
Your belly, which I touch, perhaps.
So count backward as for launching a spacecraft,
And sleep, or count forward
As to start a song, and sleep.

Let's make sweet eulogies for each other
While we lie together in the dark. Tears
Remain longer than what caused them.
The newspaper was burned to a mist
By my eyes and the wheat
Goes on growing in Pharaoh's dream.
Time is not inside the clock
And love is, sometimes, in bodies.
Words you utter out of your sleep
Are food and drink for the wild angels.
And our disheveled bed
Is the last nature reserve,
With screaming laughter and green, fat weeping.

A long time ago I wanted to tell you to sleep
And that the black night will be upholstered
With red soft velvet around all that's
Hard in you, like a case
Of geometrical instruments.

And that I shall keep you sacred like the Sabbath,
Also during working days, and that
We shall always stay together
Just as on a Happy New Year card
With a dove and the Holy Scroll
Covered with silver dust.
And that we are still cheaper
Than a computer. And that's why they'll
Not mind if we go on living.

Like the Inner Wall of a House

I found myself
Suddenly, and too early in life,
Like the inner wall of a house
Which has become an outside wall after wars and
    devastations.
I almost forget
How it is to be inside. No pain anymore,
No love. Near and far
Are both at the same distance from me
And equal.

I never imagined what happens to colors.
Their fate is man's fate: light blue still slumbers
In the memory of dark blue and night. Paleness
Sighs out of a purple dream. A wind brings smells
From far off
And itself has no smell.
And the leaves of the hatzav* die
Long before their white flower,
Which never knows
About the greenness in spring and dark love.

*Hatzav—a wild flower whose leaves grow and die in spring and whose
white flower grows only in autumn.

I lift my eyes to the mountains. Now I understand
What it means to lift eyes, what a heavy load
It is. But those hard longings,
That pain-never-again-to-be-inside!

A Czech Refugee in London

In a very short black velvet skirt,
A refugee of policies. (Her father in prison there.)
Her cunt very powerful, like the only eye
Of a war hero.
With her white thighs she walks strongly
Under this gray sky. "Each one in his time
Does his duty." With us it's
Many deserts with caves and holes to hide:
"Does the things he has to do."

She behaves here as in a schoolbook for foreign
      languages:
In the morning she gets up. She washes. (She
Doesn't think about me.) She dresses.
She comes back in the evening. She reads.
(She'll never think about me.) She sleeps.

"At the end of spring, when the air softens,
I find out every year that I'm without defenses."

Letter

To sit on the veranda of a hotel in Jerusalem
and to write: Sweetly pass the days
from desert to sea. And to write: Tears, here,
dry quickly. This little blot
is a tear that has melted ink. That's how
they wrote a hundred years ago. "I have
drawn a circle round it."

Time passes—like somebody who, on a telephone,
is laughing or weeping far away from me:
whatever I'm hearing I can't see.
And whatever I see I don't hear.

We were not careful when we said "next year"
or "a month ago." These words are like
glass splinters, which you can hurt yourself with,
or cut veins. Those who do things like that.

But you were beautiful, like the interpretation
of ancient books.
Surplus of women in your far country
brought you to me, but
other statistics have taken you
away from me.

To live is to build a ship and a harbor
at the same time. And to complete the harbor
long after the ship was drowned.

And to finish: I remember only
that there was mist. And whoever
remembers only mist—
what does he remember?

The Sweet Breakdown of Abigail

We hit her with little blows
Like an egg for peeling.

Desperate, perfume blows
She hits back at the world.

With pointed gigglings she takes revenge
For all that sadness.

And with hasty fallings-in-love,
Like hiccups of emotion.

Terrorist of sweetness,
She fills bombs
With despair and cinnamon, cloves and love splinters.

At night when she tears her jewelry
Off herself
There's great danger she won't know the limit
And will go on tearing and slashing away
All of her life.

With Sad Slyness

With sad slyness you've learned
To extract love from this world.
With the pressed and insolent voice of street urchins
You speak soft words
And your body has grown frightened hair
At its prophecy spots.

Your skin is the outer skin
Of all that has ever happened.
When I caress you at night
I caress wars and ancient kings
And whole nations wandering
Or resting at peace.

I hold your hand
In which you hold a handkerchief
In which are the tears—
The salt of all salts.

A Tall Girl and Very Precise

A tall girl with butterfly kisses
of a little child,
with earrings
to reinforce her "yes" and her "no."
A silver mezuzah cameo round her neck—
but a mezuzah brings luck only to a door.

A tall girl and very precise,
like a bell tower,
from the top down
a bell at each floor—
like the tower at Attoor
on the Mount of Olives.

She too is preparing herself
to become a beautiful landscape—
a color postcard, without me,
with the sun from behind.